TRIVIA TRACKDOWN

CHALLENGING QUESTIONS TO SHARPEN RESEARCH SKILLS
Grades 4-6

Written by Linda Schwartz
Illustrated by Beverly Armstrong

Communication & Transportation

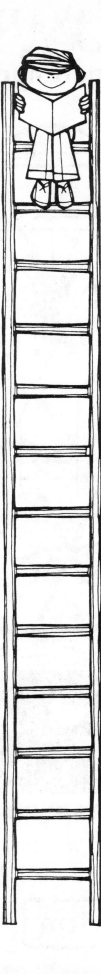

The Learning Works

Edited by Sherri M. Butterfield

The purchase of this book entitles the individual teacher to reproduce copies for use in the classroom.

The reproduction of any part for an entire school or school system or for commercial use is strictly prohibited.

No form of this work may be reproduced or transmitted or recorded without written permission from the publisher.

Trivia Trackdown
Communication & Transportation

Trivia Trackdown is a series of books in which challenging and unusual questions are used to stimulate thinking and to sharpen research skills. These books are divided into two sections, each related to a specific area of study. In each section are sets of questions covering a variety of topics. These questions vary in difficulty and are based on facts found in almanacs, atlases, dictionaries, encyclopedias, world record books, and other similar reference materials. The facts have been especially selected to interest students in grades four through six. In addition to trivia, some of these research questions deal with important facts that should also be fun to track down.

You can use the question pages in this book in any or all of the following ways:

1. Have individual students select single pages and see how quickly they can find and write the answers to all ten questions. Encourage use of classroom and library reference materials.

2. Have students work in pairs to complete one sheet or all of the sheets in a section.

3. Make **Trivia Trackdown** a team effort. Suggest that groups of three or more students compete against other groups of the same size to see who can find the answers first.

4. Allow your class to challenge another class of the same grade level to a **Trivia Trackdown** contest. Evaluate answers on the basis of accuracy, completeness, and speed, and recognize the Topnotch Trivia Trackers.

5. Color, mount, and laminate at least one copy of each page. Place these pages in a learning center with appropriate reference materials. Encourage students to explore the center during their free time and to complete question pages for extra credit or just for fun.

6. Have students compile their own booklets of trivia questions and answers.

7. Instead of using **Trivia Trackdown** pages as written exercises, hold a Trivia Bee. Ask questions aloud of individual students to find a class champion.

Other Books Available in This Series

Animals & Science
Social Studies & Famous People
Sports & Space

Contents

Name _____

Advertising

1. The English word **advertising** comes from the Latin words ***vertere***, meaning "to turn," and ***ad***, meaning "to or toward." Thus, advertising **turns** someone's attention **toward** a person, place, product, service, or idea. What was probably the first form of advertising?

    _____

2. In 1841, an enterprising man started the first advertising agency in the United States. Name this man. _____

3. Each year, an average of how much money is spent per person on advertising in the United States? _____

4. Name the six chief advertising media. _____

    _____

5. Name the medium in which the most advertising dollars are spent. _____

6. U.S. newspapers devote approximately what percentage of their space to advertising?

    _____

7. What is the most widely used form of outdoor advertising? _____

8. In some advertisements, a person endorses a product. What are these advertisements called? _____

9. Which U.S. presidential campaign was the first to be directed by advertising executives rather than by politicians? _____

10. Which U.S. government agency enforces federal laws against deceptive advertising? __

    _____

Name _____

Braille

1. **Braille** is a specialized writing system in which arrangements of raised dots are used to represent letters. Name the blind French student who invented this system. _____

   _____

2. How old was he at the time? _____

3. Where did he get the idea for this remarkable writing system? _____

   _____

4. In what year was this writing system first published? _____

5. This writing system is based on cells, or groups, of dots. What is the largest number of dots that a braille cell can contain? _____

6. By varying the numbers and positions of dots within each cell, how many different arrangements can be created? _____

7. Words written in letters are read with the eyes. With what part of the body is braille read?

   _____

8. Although the dots within a single braille cell usually stand for letters, in some instances they may stand for a frequently used word. When all of the positions within a cell are filled by dots, the reader understands that this arrangement means what? _____

9. Name the six-key machine that is similar to a typewriter and is used to write braille.

   _____

10. In 1961, the *World Book Encylopedia* was translated into braille. Of how many volumes did this encyclopedia consist? _____

Name _____

Communication Potpourri

1. What and where was the earliest known library? _____

    _____

2. Who invented movable type? _____

3. Which Italian inventor is known as the "father of radio"? _____

4. What was the name of the first magazine published in the United States? _____

    _____

5. In what year did U.S. motion pictures become "talkies"? _____

6. In what year did commercial television begin operation in the United States? _____

7. Which artificial satellite first relayed television programs between the United States and

    Europe? _____

8. Name the first commercial communications satellite. _____

9. Residents of which nation make the most telephone calls per person? _____

10. Sometimes, messages are written in a secret code. What name is given to the process of

    encoding and decoding messages? _____

Name _____

Computers

1. There are two basic types of computers. Name them. _____

   _____

2. How many digits form the basis of the numerical system on which the development of today's computers was based? _____

3. How many **bits** are in a **byte**? _____

4. In 1944, Howard Aiken worked with International Business Machines (IBM) to develop a calculator that used electrical relays and punched tape. What was this calculator called?

   _____

5. What was the name of the first electronic digital computer? _____

6. In what year did Sperry-Rand build UNIVAC? _____

7. What is a set of instructions for a computer called? _____

8. What is a **bug** in a computer program? _____

9. Name the most widely used computer language. _____

10. **COBOL** is the name of one computer language. This name is an **acronym**, that is, a word formed from the initial letter or letters of longer words. What are the longer words from which the word COBOL is formed? _____

    _____

Name _____

Mail

1. Name the Roman emperor who established a highly organized mail delivery system in ancient times. _____

2. In what city was the first official postal system established in the American colonies?

   _____

3. Who was the first American postmaster general? _____

4. Overland mail was carried by stagecoach from Missouri to California. How many days did this two-thousand-mile journey take? _____

5. On April 3, 1860, the first Pony Express riders carried mail from Sacramento, California, to St. Joseph, Missouri. About how long did this trip take? _____

6. In 1911, an American pilot made the first official airmail flight in the United States. Name this pilot. _____

7. In what year was the zip code introduced?

   _____

8. What do the letters in the acronym **ZIP** stand for? _____

   _____

9. In 1971, an independent agency was established to operate the postal system in the United States. Name this agency. _____

   _____

10. Where does mail that cannot be delivered or returned go? _____

Name _____

Newspapers

1. Who founded the first newspaper in the American colonies? _____

2. What was the name of this newspaper? _____

   _____

3. During the early 1900s, an American journalist and publisher amassed a fortune as pro-
   prietor of a newspaper chain and publishing empire, and built a castle in San Simeon,
   California. Name this man. _____

4. Seven prizes are awarded annually by Columbia University for editorial writing; for local,
   national, and international reporting; for the best cartoon; for the best news photograph;
   and for distinguished and meritorious public service. These prizes are named for an im-
   migrant journalist and newspaper publisher. What are these prizes called and for whom
   were they named? _____

5. Which country leads the world in newspaper readership? _____

6. About what percent of all U.S. dailies belong to newspaper chains? _____

7. Name the largest newspaper chain in the United States. _____

8. What are the two major formats of newspapers? _____

9. A color is used to describe journalism that features sensational or scandalous stories or
   gives a sensational twist to ordinary news. Name this color. _____

10. What is the opening paragraph of a news story called? _____

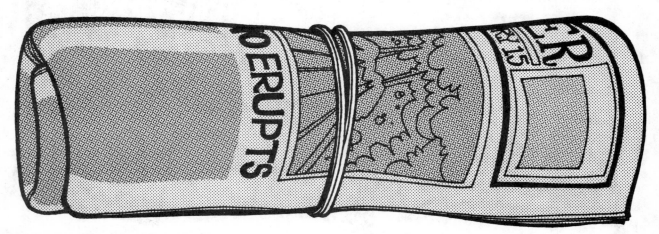

Name _____

Radio

1. Who was the first person to send radio communication signals through the air? ____
   _____

2. A radio works by changing sound waves into radio waves. What is another name for radio waves? _____

3. Sound waves travel at the rate of about one-fifth mile per second. At what rate do radio waves travel? _____

4. Which part of a radio enables a listener to select particular frequencies? _____

5. What is the scientific term for the number of times an electric wave vibrates each second?
   _____

6. For what does the acronym **FM** stand? _____

7. What name is given to the initials that identify a radio station? _____

8. The federal government issued the first license to broadcast regularly to station WBZ in Springfield, Massachusetts. On what date was this license issued? _____

9. Name the two actors who were better known to millions of listeners as Amos and Andy during the Golden Age of radio. _____

10. What is the operator of an amateur radio station called? _____

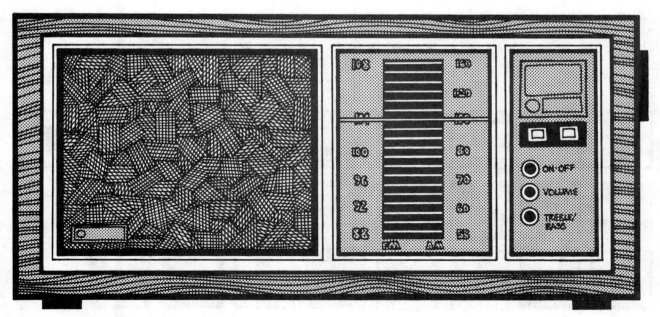

Signaling

1. What are the three main methods of signaling? _____

_____

2. Visual signaling is often done with flags. How many flags are used to send semaphore

signals? _____

3. Colored flags hanging from crosspieces on the masts of ships are used to send which

types of signals? _____

4. Name the code used by sailors to send the signals described in question 3. _____

_____

5. What does flying a national flag upside down signal? _____

6. The word that is sent over voice radio as a distress signal probably came from the French

term **m'aider**, meaning "help me." What is this famous international distress signal? __

_____

7. What letters make up the radio telegraph distress signal? _____

8. What name is given to the special, deep-voiced sirens used on lighthouses and ships?

_____

9. Name the floating markers that are operated by the motion of the sea and may produce

a sound as a warning signal to ships. _____

10. Enemy submarines can be detected by signals from an echo-sounding device. Name this

device. _____

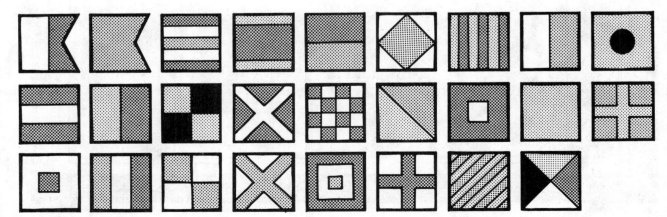

Name _____

Sign Language

1. What is a sign language? _____

_____

2. For what purposes is a sign language used? _____

_____

_____

3. Who was the first deaf person to teach other deaf people in the United States? ____

_____

4. Where was the first American school for the deaf established? _____

5. American Sign Language is not based on letters or on words. On what is it based?

_____

6. What acronym is commonly used to stand for American Sign Language? _____

7. What is another name for the American manual alphabet? _____

8. How many hand symbols does this alphabet contain? _____

9. In the American manual alphabet, what does this sign represent?

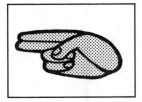   _____

10. Different tribes of Plains Indians spoke different languages. Because they were unable to understand one another, they developed a sign language in which they could communicate easily. In this language, what idea were the Indians communicating when they held the back of the right hand to the lips, clasped the ring and little finger with the thumb, and spread the first two fingers? _____

Symbols

1. What is a **symbol**? _____
   _____

2. During the eighteenth century, John Arbuthnot, a British writer, wit, and scientist, created a series of satirical pamphlets. From a bluff, kindhearted, bullheaded farmer described in these pamphlets comes the national nickname for an Englishman and a symbol for Great Britain. Name this symbol. _____

3. During the war of 1812, a bearded male figure formally dressed in national colors came to represent the United States. Name this familiar figure. _____

4. Which country has a maple leaf as its symbol? _____

5. Which country has a bear as its symbol? _____

6. The fleur-de-lis is the symbol of which country? _____

7. In the United States, which animal is a symbol for the Republican Party? _____
   _____

8. What is the symbol for Judaism? _____

9. A heart is the symbol for which emotion? _____

10. What does this symbol mean?

 _____

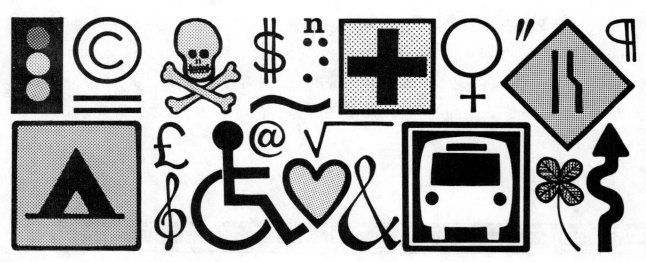

Telephone

1. The English word **telephone** comes from two Greek words, **tele** and **phone**. What do these Greek words mean? _____

    _____

2. Alexander Graham Bell invented the first successful telephone in 1876. In what city did he do so? _____

3. What were the first words spoken over the telephone? _____

    _____

4. In 1877, a banker named Roswell C. Downer installed the first commercial telephone line between his home and his bank. Over what distance did this line extend? _____

    _____

5. In what year were dial telephones first used? _____

6. In 1970, International Direct Distance Dialing (IDDD) began operating between which two cities?_____

7. Name the two main parts of a telephone. _____

8. Which one of these parts converts sound into a pattern of electric waves that can travel over a wire? _____

9. Telephone calls made to ships at sea are transmitted by means of what type of waves?

    _____

10. Telephone calls are classified as local and long distance. What percentage of the calls made in the United States are local? _____

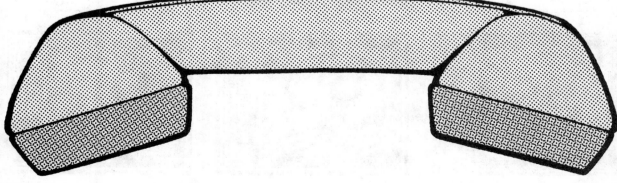

Name _____

Television

1. The English word **television** comes from the Greek word **_tele_** and the Latin word **_videre_**. What do these two words mean?_____

   _____

2. There are three national television networks in the United States. Name them. _____

   _____

   _____

3. Which federal government agency regulates television broadcasting in the United States?

   _____

4. On the average, a television set is in use in each home in the United States for how many hours a day? _____

5. Which television entertainer was the star of *The Texaco Star Theater* and became the first TV personality to attract a huge, nationwide audience? _____

6. Who was emcee for the popular TV variety show called *The Toast of the Town*?

   _____

7. In what year were color telecasts first introduced? _____

8. A communications satellite launched in 1965 made worldwide television broadcasting possible. Name this satellite. _____

9. Name the mechanical device that helps forgetful television actors remember their lines.

   _____

10. What is a **wipe**? _____

    _____

Answer Key

Page 5, Advertising
1. outdoor signs above shop doors
2. Volney B. Palmer
3. $155
4. direct mail, magazines, newspapers, outdoor signs, radio, and television
5. newspapers
6. 60 percent
7. billboards *or* posters
8. testimonials
9. the 1952 campaign of Dwight D. Eisenhower
10. the Federal Trade Commission

Page 6, Braille
1. Louis Braille
2. fifteen years old
3. from a dot-dash code used for sending messages to soldiers at night
4. 1829
5. six
6. sixty-three
7. the fingertips
8. for
9. a braillewriter
10. 145

Page 7, Communication Potpourri
1. a collection of clay tablets in Babylonia in the twenty-first century B.C.
2. Johannes Gutenberg
3. Guglielmo Marconi
4. *The American Magazine*
5. 1927
6. 1941
7. Telstar I
8. Early Bird
9. Canada
10. cryptography

Page 8, Computers
1. analog and digital
2. two
3. eight
4. the Mark I
5. ENIAC
6. 1951
7. a program
8. an error *or* a mistake
9. BASIC
10. COmmon Business Oriented Language

Page 9, Mail
1. Augustus Caesar
2. Boston, Massachusetts
3. Benjamin Franklin
4. twenty-five
5. eight to ten days
6. Earle Ovington
7. 1963
8. Zoning Improvement Plan
9. the United States Postal Service
10. to the Dead-Mail Office

Page 10, Newspapers
1. Benjamin Harris of Boston
2. *Publick Occurrences Both Foreign and Domestick*
3. William Randolph Hearst
4. the Pulitzer Prizes named for Joseph Pulitzer
5. Sweden
6. 60 percent
7. Gannett Newspapers
8. standard and tabloid
9. yellow
10. a lead

Answer Key
(continued)

Page 11, Radio
1. Guglielmo Marconi
2. electromagnetic waves
3. 186,282 miles per second
4. the tuner
5. frequency
6. frequency modulation
7. call letters *or* call signs
8. September 15, 1921
9. Freeman Gosden and Charles Correll
10. a ham

Page 12, Signaling
1. electrical, sound, and visual
2. two
3. flaghoist signals
4. International Flag Code
5. distress
6. Mayday
7. SOS
8. foghorns
9. buoys
10. sonar

Page 13, Sign Language
1. a system of gestures and hand signals used to communicate words and ideas
2. to communicate with people who cannot understand a spoken language because they speak another language or are hearing-impaired or deaf
3. a Frenchman named Laurent Clerc
4. in Hartford, Connecticut
5. ideas
6. AMESLAN *or* Ameslan
7. finger alphabet *or* finger spelling
8. twenty-six
9. the letter *h*
10. forked tongue *or* two tongues, which meant a lie, a falsehood, or deceit

Page 14, Symbols
1. anything that communicates a fact or idea or that stands for an object or concept
2. John Bull
3. Uncle Sam
4. Canada
5. Russia
6. France
7. an elephant
8. the six-pointed Star of David
9. love
10. no *or* don't

Page 15, Telephone
1. *Tele* means "at a distance," and *phone* means "sound." Thus, the telephone is a device that enables sound to be heard at a distance, or far away.
2. Boston, Massachusetts
3. "Mr. Watson, come here. I want you!"
4. three miles
5. 1896
6. New York and London
7. transmitter and receiver
8. the transmitter
9. radio *or* electromagnetic
10. more than 90 percent

Page 16, Television
1. *Tele* means "at a distance," and *videre* means "to see." Thus, television is a device that enables viewers to see things that happen at a distance, or far away.
2. the American Broadcasting Companies (ABC), the Columbia Broadcasting System (CBS), and the National Broadcasting Company (NBC)
3. the Federal Communications Commission (FCC)
4. six hours
5. Milton Berle
6. Ed Sullivan
7. 1953
8. Early Bird
9. a teleprompter
10. a special effect in which one picture appears to push another off the television screen

Name _____

Airplanes

1. What was the name of the biplane in which Orville and Wilbur Wright made the first engine-powered, heavier-than-air flight? _____

2. Which Italian artist and inventor made drawings of flying machines approximately four hundred years before the Wright Brothers' flight? _____

3. Which two Americans made the first airplane flight across the North Pole in 1926?

   _____

4. Who made the first solo nonstop transatlantic flight in 1927? _____

5. In 1932, an American became the first woman to make a solo flight across the Atlantic Ocean. Who was this woman? _____

6. What flamboyant aviator designed, built, and flew the world's largest plane in 1947?

   _____

7. Today, this wooden airplane is on display in Long Beach, California. What is this plane called? _____

8. On October 14, 1947, a U.S. Air Force pilot made the first supersonic flight in a rocket-powered airplane. Name this famous test pilot. _____

9. In 1970, the first jumbo jet entered airline service. What is this gigantic plane called?

   _____

10. Which two countries built the Concorde, a supersonic transport? _____

    _____

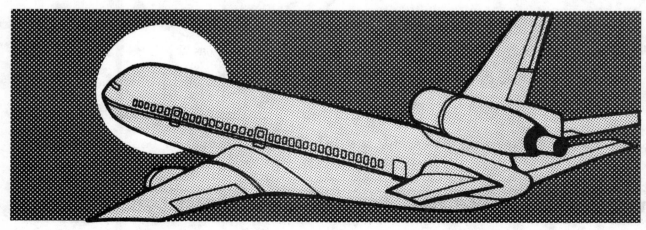

Name _____

Airships

1. An **airship** is a lighter-than-air craft that, unlike a hot-air balloon, flies under its own power and can be easily steered. Airships are sometimes called **dirigibles**, from the Latin word *dirigere*. What does this Latin word mean? _____

    _____

2. Cigar-shaped airships are sometimes called **zeppelins**. For whom are they named?

    _____

3. From 1910 to 1914, the world's first airline carried mail and about 35,000 passengers between German cities. Name this airline. _____

4. Which U.S. Navy airship, first flown in 1924, became known as the "queen of the air"?

    _____

5. In 1929, an airship flew around the world, becoming the only one ever to do so. Name this airship. _____

6. On May 6, 1937, a tragedy ended regular airship service between Germany and the United States. What was this tragedy? _____

    _____

7. How many successful flights had the *Hindenburg* made across the Atlantic Ocean? __

    _____

8. Hydrogen, the lightest gas available, was once used to fill the gas bags on airships. Today, it has been replaced by helium. What is the primary advantage of helium? _____

    _____

9. Airships are also called **blimps**. The world's largest blimp was the U.S. Navy ZPG-3W, which first flew in July 1958. When and by what was this airship destroyed? _____

    _____

10. What name is given to the car that is suspended from the hull, or body, of an airship?

    _____

Name _____

Automobiles

1. What kind of engines powered the first road vehicles that could travel by themselves?

    _____

2. In the United States, the most famous of these vehicles were manufactured between 1897 and 1924 and named for their builders, Francis E. and Freelan O. Stanley. What were these cars called? _____

3. In 1885, the first successful gasoline engine was developed. In which country did this development take place? _____

4. Two men, experimenting separately in that country, built gasoline engines similar to those that are in use today. What are the names of these two men? _____

    _____

5. Name the two brothers who established the first American company for the manufacture of gasoline automobiles in 1895. _____

6. A fire that destroyed one American auto plant led to the creation of the first automobile assembly line and the first mass-produced automobile. Name this automobile. _____

    _____

7. Which was the first car with interchangeable parts? _____

8. Which U.S. automaker used conveyor belts and improved assembly line methods to cut production time for a single automobile from 12½ hours to 1½ hours? _____

9. How much did a Ford Model T sell for in 1916? _____

10. Which city is known as the "automobile capital of the world"? _____

Name _____

Balloons

1. A **balloon** is an airtight bag that is filled with gas. Why is a balloon able to rise? __

_____

2. Three different gases are used in balloons. Name them. _____

3. Two brothers are given credit for being the first Europeans to make a balloon that success-

fully carried a person. Name these brothers. _____

_____

4. An American doctor named John Jefferies and a Frenchman named Jean-Pierre

Blanchard flew across the English Channel in a hydrogen balloon. On what day did they

make their historic flight? _____

5. Ballooning began in the United States when Blanchard went up in a balloon on

January 9, 1793, before a large crowd that included President George Washington. From

which city was this ascent made? _____

6. Who was the first person to drop leaflets from a balloon? _____

7. Of what material are most balloons made today? _____

8. Near the top of a balloon, there is a long seam that can be opened quickly when the balloon

lands to let gases escape. What is this seam called? _____

9. An early American balloon pilot invented this seam. What was his name? _____

_____

10. The James Gordon Bennett Cup was awarded nearly every year from 1906 until World

War II to the winner of an international balloon distance race. Who was the first winner

of this cup? _____

Name _____

Bicycles

1. The first bicycle, called a **célérifère**, was invented about 1790 by Comte Mede de Sivrac of France. What did it look like? _____

2. The **draisine**, invented about 1816, was a two-wheeled vehicle that the rider straddled. It had no pedals, so the rider walked and pushed it uphill but sat on it to coast downhill. Who invented the *draisine*? _____

3. A French carriage maker obtained the first U.S. patent on a pedal-powered bicycle in 1866. What was his name? _____

4. Name the bicycle, popular in the late nineteenth century, that had a huge front wheel and a small rear wheel. _____

5. What was the chief advantage of this bicycle? _____

_____

_____

_____

6. What did J. K. Starley produce? _____

_____

7. Most lightweight bicycles have what type of brakes? _____

8. What name is given to a bicycle that carries two riders? _____

9. What does a **derailleur** derail? _____

_____

s 10. In which year did bicycle racing, or cycling, first become a recognized event in the Olympic Games? _____

Name _____

Boats

1. Name the leading boating nation. _____

2. What are the two main kinds of pleasure boats? _____

3. How are sailboats classified? _____

   _____

4. What name is given to pleasure boats that are more than thirty feet long? _____

5. What are boats with three hulls called? _____

6. What name is given to a fast-traveling boat designed to take advantage of the lift created by metal wing-shaped structures and to skim over the surface of the water? _____

   _____

7. What is the left side of a boat called? _____

8. What is the right side of a boat called? _____

9. Where and when was the first U.S. yacht club organized? _____

10. In the United States, which group is responsible for enforcing federal boating laws and regulations? _____

Bonus Question

What does the word **posh** mean and what is its possible, though unproved, connection with boating?

Name _____

Helicopters

1. The English word **helicopter** comes from the Greek words **helix** and **pteron**. What do these two Greek words mean? _____

2. Aviation historians disagree on who made the first manned helicopter flight. Which two men are usually given credit for this accomplishment? _____

3. In 1939, a Russian engineer, who had come to the United States twenty years before, built the first practical single-rotor helicopter. What was his name? _____

4. The world's first helicopter airline operated from 1947 to 1962. Name this airline. __ _____

5. The world speed record for a helicopter was set on September 21, 1978. What is this record speed? _____

6. Where and by whom was this record set? _____

7. Between September 1 and September 30, 1982, H. Ross Perot and Jay Coburn made the first around-the-world flight in a helicopter. What was the name of their aircraft? _____

8. Between August 5, 1982, and July 22, 1983, a pilot from Australia made the first solo round-the-world flight in a helicopter. What was his name? _____

9. What type of helicopter has a rotor at each end of its body? _____

10. What is the largest helicopter? _____

Name _____

Motorcycles

1. The earliest real motorcycle was a wooden-framed vehicle built during October and November 1885 by a German engineer. Name this engineer. _____

2. From which vehicle was this motorcycle developed? _____

3. What was the name of this first motorcycle? _____

4. The first motorcycle race was held on an oval track at Sheen House, Richmond, Surrey, England. What was the date of this race? _____

5. Charles Jarrott won this race. What make of cycle was he riding? _____

6. What are the two main types of motorcycles? _____

   _____

7. Which organization governs motorcycle competition in the United States? _____

   _____

8. Which organization governs international motorcycle competition? _____

   _____

9. On August 28, 1978, motorcyclist Donald Vesco made two runs over the Bonneville Salt Flats in Utah in which he set AMA and FIM absolute speed records. What was the average speed of his faster run? _____

10. Which country manufactures the most motorcycles? _____

Name _____

Rockets

1. A **rocket** is a device that is propelled through the air as a result of the rearward discharge of gases produced by burning fuel. What is the scientific term for the forward push given a rocket by this rearward discharge? _____

2. Which ancient people probably invented rockets? _____

3. Which American scientist is known as the father of modern rockets? _____
   _____

4. Which German rocket expert directed the development of the powerful V-2 rocket during World War II? _____

5. On October 14, 1947, a U.S. Air Force pilot used a rocket-powered airplane to make the first supersonic flight. Name this famous test pilot. _____

6. What was this rocket-powered plane called? _____

7. What kind of rocket was used to launch the first American satellite, Explorer I, into orbit?
   _____

8. What kind of rocket was used to carry the first astronauts to the moon? _____
   _____

9. How much fuel does this powerful rocket burn in the first 2¾ minutes of flight? _____
   _____

10. The lyrics of a famous song speak of how a flag was visible in "the rockets' red glare." What is the title of this song? _____

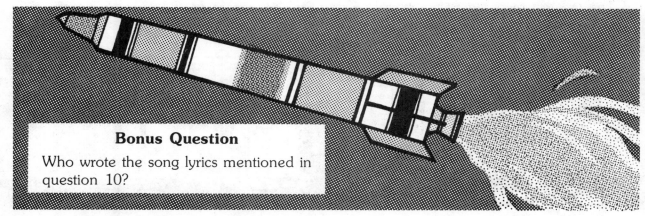

Bonus Question

Who wrote the song lyrics mentioned in question 10?

Trains

1. Which Englishman is given credit for having invented the steam locomotive? _____

   _____

2. Which American inventor and cabinetmaker designed and patented a train car with folding

   upper berths and extendable seat cushions to make lower berths? _____

3. Which train station is the oldest in the world? _____

4. On May 10, 1869, a golden spike was driven to mark the completion of the world's first

   transcontinental rail line. Which two cities were connected by this line? _____

   _____

5. Built between 1903 and 1913, the world's largest train station covers forty-eight acres on

   two levels and has sixty-five tracks. Identify this station. _____

   _____

6. In 1934, the first streamlined diesel-electric passenger train began service in the United

   States. What was this train called? _____

7. The highest standard gauge train track in the world is on the Peruvian State Railways at

   La Cima. How far above sea level is this track? _____

8. Which rail system is the busiest in the world? _____

9. A record for the world's fastest rail speed with passengers aboard was set in December

   1979 by a Maglev test train in Miyazaki, Japan. What was this record speed? _____

   _____

10. The greatest recorded train robbery occurred on August 8, 1963. In which country did

    this robbery take place? _____

Name _____

Transportation Potpourri

1. Who built the first system of paved roads? _____

2. Around 1450, invention of the three-masted ship made sailing against the wind much easier. Who invented this ship? _____

3. In 1662, Blaise Pascal gave Paris the first public mass transportation system when he invented the **omnibus**. What was an *omnibus*? _____

4. The first air crossing of the English Channel in a balloon took how many hours? _____

5. Which oceangoing vessels of the 1800s were the fastest sailing ships ever built? _____
   _____

6. Name the ship that was the first to cross the Atlantic Ocean entirely under steam power.
   _____

7. In 1860, a Frenchman built the first practical gasoline engine for a road vehicle. Name this Frenchman. _____

8. Where and when was the first successful subway built? _____
   _____

9. Name the German company that built and flew the first jet airplane. _____
   _____

10. Which private corporation took over the operation of most passenger trains in the United States in 1971? _____

Name _____

Wagons

1. Who were among the first people to use wagons? _____

2. Chariots were two-wheeled vehicles that were lighter and faster than early wagons. By whom were chariots developed? _____

3. In which European country was the four-wheeled coach developed during the Middle Ages?

   _____

4. Name the wagon built by the German farmers of Pennsylvania. _____

   _____

5. What kind of wagon carried pioneers westward over the Allegheny Mountains from the early 1700s until about 1850? _____

6. Where did this wagon get its name? _____

7. What were these wagons sometimes called? _____

8. What U.S. president was in office when stagecoaches first began to travel colonial roads?

   _____

9. In which year did Congress begin mail service by stagecoach? _____

10. What was the name of the popular open American carriage of the early 1900s which was used for short business and pleasure trips? _____

Answer Key

Page 19, Airplanes
1. *Flyer*
2. Leonardo da Vinci
3. Richard E. Byrd and Floyd Bennett
4. Charles A. Lindbergh
5. Amelia Earhart
6. Howard Hughes
7. the *Spruce Goose*
8. Charles E. Yeager
9. a Boeing 747
10. Great Britain and France

Page 20, Airships
1. "to set in a straight line; to aim, direct, or steer"
2. Count Ferdinand von Zeppelin of Germany
3. the German Airship Transportation Company
4. the *Los Angeles*
5. the *Graf Zeppelin*
6. The *Hindenburg's* hydrogen-filled gas bag burst into flames and exploded, killing thirty-six persons.
7. thirty-six
8. Safety. Helium is inert and will not burn.
9. in February 1960 by a gust of wind
10. gondola

Page 21, Automobiles
1. steam engines
2. Stanley steamers
3. Germany
4. Gottlieb Daimler and Karl Benz
5. Charles E. Duryea and J. Frank Duryea
6. the 1901 Oldsmobile
7. the 1908 Cadillac
8. Henry Ford
9. $400
10. Detroit, Michigan

Page 22, Balloons
1. because the particular gas it contains is lighter than the surrounding air
2. hydrogen, helium, and coal gas
3. Jacques Étienne Montgolfier and Joseph Michel Montgolfier
4. January 7, 1785
5. Philadelphia, Pennsylvania
6. Charles Ferson Durant
7. plastic
8. the ripping seam *or* the ripping panel
9. John Wise
10. Frank P. Lahm of the United States

Page 23, Bicycles
1. a wooden scooter
2. Baron Karl von Drais of Germany
3. Pierre Lallement
4. high-wheeler *or* penny farthing
5. This bicycle offered a mechanical advantage. Because the front wheel had a large circumference and the pedals were attached to it, this bicycle traveled a long way for each turn of the pedals.
6. the first commercially successful safety bicycle
7. caliper brakes
8. tandem
9. the chain from one gear to another
10. 1896

Page 24, Boats
1. the United States of America
2. motorboats and sailboats
3. according to the way in which their sails are rigged, or arranged
4. yachts
5. trimarans
6. hydrofoil
7. port
8. starboard
9. in New York City in 1844
10. the U.S. Coast Guard
Bonus: The word **posh** means "elegant, fashionable, deluxe, swanky." The letters **POSH** were used on the manifests of luxury ocean liners to indicate which passengers were traveling **port out, starboard home**, the most desirable stateroom placement because it was on the shady side.

Answer Key
(continued)

Page 25, Helicopters

1. *Helix* means "spiral," and *pteron* means "wing."
2. Paul Cornu and Louis Bréguet
3. Igor I. Sikorsky
4. Los Angeles Airways
5. 228.9 miles per hour
6. near Moscow, USSR, by Gourguen Karapetyan
7. the *Spirit of Texas*
8. Dick Smith
9. a tandem helicopter
10. The Soviet Mil Mi-12 ("Homer"), also known as the V-12

Page 26, Motorcycles

1. Gottlieb Daimler
2. the bicycle
3. the *Einspur*
4. November 29, 1897
5. a Fournier
6. those built for use on paved surfaces, or roads, and those built for off-road use
7. the American Motorcycle Association (AMA)
8. the Fédération Internationale Motocycliste (FIM)
9. 318.66 miles per hour
10. Japan

Page 27, Rockets

1. thrust
2. the Chinese
3. Robert H. Goddard
4. Wernher von Braun
5. Charles E. Yeager
6. the X-1
7. a Juno I rocket
8. a Saturn V rocket
9. 560,000 gallons
10. "The Star-Spangled Banner"
Bonus: Francis Scott Key

Page 28, Trains

1. Richard Trevithick
2. George Mortimer Pullman
3. the Liverpool Road Station in Manchester, England, which was first used in 1830
4. Sacramento, California, and Omaha, Nebraska
5. Grand Central Terminal in New York City, which is also called Grand Central Station
6. the Burlington *Zephyr*
7. 15,806 feet
8. Japanese National Railways
9. 321.2 miles per hour
10. England

Page 29, Transportation Potpourri

1. the Romans
2. the Portuguese
3. a horse-drawn wagon used to carry passengers
4. two
5. clipper ships
6. the *Sirius*
7. Jean Étienne Lenoir
8. in London, England, in 1863
9. the Heinkel Company
10. Amtrack

Page 30, Wagons

1. the Egyptians
2. the Greeks and the Romans
3. Germany
4. the prairie schooner
5. the Conestoga wagon
6. from the Conestoga Valley in Pennsylvania, where it was built
7. the "camels of the prairies"
8. George Washington
9. 1785
10. the New England buckboard wagon

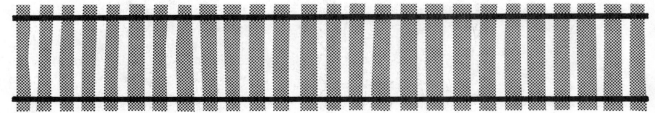